SANCTIONED

MARY SUSAN SPENCER CUMINALE

Olympus Story House

Table of Contents

It doesn't matter what you do in life,
It's who you are in life.

I was working for the American Red Cross as a phlebotomy nurse (the person who would stick your arm with an 18-gauge needle for a pint of blood). Every day was a different schedule, hour-wise and location-wise. Initially, I worked three days a week, and it was enjoyable work traveling throughout western New York State. Eventually, I needed to go full-time as I now maintained the health coverage for my entire family. Some days I was scheduled in corporate facilities like Xerox and Kodak; some were in a little burg town down in a musty church basement thirty-five miles away, and also, not my favorite, numerous high schools.

You see, drawing a pint of blood on a junior or senior was tricky, as they often hadn't had anything to eat or drink since the night before, including nothing for breakfast, so it was difficult to find their veins due to borderline dehydration. However, this was not the only difficulty. I called it "Monkey See, Monkey Do Syndrome." One student would faint, and when others witnessed their friends fainting one by one, they followed suit, so to speak. Many times, we hadn't even touched them with a needle!

Well, one day down in Corning, New York, we held a blood drive, which was advertised and shot live for television. I must say, it was a bit unnerving to insert an 18-gauge needle into someone's arm with a camera on you. This Corning, New York, blood drive was a ten-hour blood drive standing on your feet, plus three hours travel in each direction. I will also mention it was my turn to drive the Red Cross van with all the blood we had collected, plus five of my fellow nurses, back home to Rochester, New York, in a snowstorm. No, no pressure.

So when I safely arrived home at 10:00 p.m., I found my eleven-year- old son in the basement playing, all the lights in the house were on, and my daughter was not home at fifteen years old. My son said he thought she was with her friends down the street. I called and told her to immediately come home. It was a school night! Where was my husband? One word: alcoholism.

Did you ever have a moment that absolutely defined your future? This was that moment. So without describing all the painful moments of obtaining a legal separation, I'll leave it to say I had to get out. I found an apartment with three bedrooms and moved in with my son. My daughter, however, at the last moment, refused to move in as she believed she wouldn't be able to complete her junior and senior years at the school she loved. Not true. My daughter was extremely active at school. Show choir and being in musicals were two of her favorite before- and after-school functions, and they were her life at that time.

In any case, I was unable to continue with my job at the Red Cross due to the extremely variable hours that changed every day. I was determined to have my son complete his year at the private school he was attending. There was a bus, but it stopped at two different schools before it arrived at his school. This took two hours both going and coming home—four hours a day, quite a lot of time—even though his school was only a little over a mile away. It was on a very busy road, and I didn't expect him to walk. I know, I know. When my grandmother was a kid, she used to walk five miles to school and home again, every day, up and down hills in blinding snowstorms. I needed to drivehim and pick him up every day. Now what? I resigned from my job. Now I was desperate and prayed, "Lord, I need to put food on the table and pay this rent. Please help me." And

He sure did. I marched into the Merry Maids and explained my situation, begged for a job, and they hired me on the spot. She said, dry your eyes and you can start tomorrow. I was assured I would get paid something that very Friday. Thank you, Lord!

Tomorrow came. I drove my son to school and went on to my new job. It kept me busy on my hands and knees; the girls always gave me, the new girl, the bathroom to scrub. Lovely. I learned a little Spanish, and they learned a little English. I did that job every day until the end of the school year.

My next job was selling grave plots, mausoleum spots, and urns. No, I'm not kidding. It was an upgrade from toilets. Training lasted a week, and then they sent me out into my own neighborhood to canvass. I sent out flyers beforehand and telephoned also, saying that I would be in their area a certain week. If they didn't immediately hang up on me, that was a potential customer. The next step would be to knock on people's doors at dinner times randomly with no set time— and they would let me in! Others, of course, closed the door promptly. Sometimes they would offer me coffee, etc. I was able to do this part of the job in the evening while my son was doing his homework, and I wouldn't be gone too long from home.

I still find that so incredible for 1994. Nonetheless, I sold them urns and grave plots and/or a spot in the mausoleum. I had a few jokes like, "If you prefer a coffee can, I have a few extra Chock-Full O' Nuts tin coffee cans," or "If you know a different way not to die at some point, fill me in." It's always better to plan whenever you can, and I believe that to this day. It helps the family to not have to make the decisions for you. After my little presentation, that's when generally the husband would saunter in from the living room (where they were always listening) and write the check. Some even kept in touch for a while, sending Christmas cards. I never was invited to funerals, thank God. It was a pretty good commission-only job that paid some of the bills and put food on the table. I never received any support.

Then came another life-defining moment. I received a phone call from a nurse friend who told me about a job involving ventilators, and she asked what experience I had. "Absolutely none," was my reply, adding, "but I'm willing to learn." A couple of days later, I arrived at the hospital as previously scheduled for an interview and went directly to the patient's room. There, standing against the back wall, were seven RNs. We were facing the patient, Dr. M., who was a neurologist, toxicologist, and psychologist. He had Lou Gehrig's disease, also known as ALS. It is a progressive neuromuscular condition that slowly renders the individual paralyzed. It is a life sentence with no cure, and in most cases lasts approximately two years. The brain is not affected. Dr. M. had been put on a ventilator as he no longer had the strength to breathe on his own. Normally, someone with this disease would never be put on a ventilator; however, as God would have it, a fellow neurologist friend stopped in to visit and found him struggling to breathe, and 911 was called.

As he stared at us from his bed, the respiratory therapist stood to the left of his bed with the vent between them. He then proceeded to give us all a one-hour verbal instruction on the LP10 vent. It was a long hour filled with terms like PIP and PEEP, this hose and that hose, and on and on. When he had finished his training, he then asked, "Does anyone have any questions?" No one spoke.

Finally, I gathered my strength and said, "I have a question. Could you start all over again from the beginning?"

Everyone chuckled except Dr. M. He said, "Everyone out! My life depends on this machine! Everyone out but you." He pointed to me and said, "You're hired."

With those two life-defining small words spoken, it took me on a journey that I never could have imagined or anticipated in any way. Praise God, I am back to my love of nursing.

I went back to the hospital several times to fully learn and feel secure with the operation of the ventilator. After all, Dr. M.'s life truly did depend on it. He was also on four liters of oxygen and needed suctioning through his tracheostomy site. For those of you who are not in the medical field, it's basically an opening in the throat where a tube is placed to keep it open. Dr. M. was fortunate to have something called a Passe Muir Valve, made in France, which allowed him to speak in his own voice. This was a brilliant product that acted like an epiglottis, and as the wind passed over it—voilà—speech. Suctioning was done on demand, as we say, as needed, as he didn't have the muscle strength to cough. No need to describe this except to say a catheter was gently placed into the windpipe to remove secretions. Too much? Won't go any further on this subject. The ventilator would usually let me know by sounding an alarm; however, there were times when Dr. M. would simply ring his bell, which was attached to the bedrail, and I would come running. At this point, he still had some use of one arm.

So now I somehow offered to prepare for his arrival home from the hospital. I'm not sure who I thought I was. Maybe wackadoodle? Yet everything seemed to fall into place over time, as God would have it. I assessed his home, and the first thing I noticed was there was absolutely no way to get him into or out of the house in a wheelchair. So I called a friend of mine who said he could build a wooden ramp at the back door ASAP. Click off one problem. Next was ordering the electric hospital bed, mattress, linens, and the like. I decided on placing the bed in the living room, as it was a bright, sunny room with a fireplace and where Dr. M. could observe traffic and walkers going by on both streets from three different windows. His home was on a corner lot with a big sycamore tree in the yard that he could also admire.

The next task was cleaning out the cupboards, the refrigerator, the stove, the range, and washing all the dishes, as a few mice had set up residence. I washed a few windows and mopped the floors just for fun. Basic cleanliness. OH, and lest I forget, the bathroom. I just can't seem to get away from cleaning other people's toilets! This all took approximately a week. The biggest problem now was for the nursing agency to find help for the remaining hours of twenty-four-hour care, seven days a week.

It was then the truth came out. I am an LPN (licensed practical nurse), not an RN. No one inquired, so I didn't offer. They were left with no choice but to hire me officially with the nursing agency and give me LPN wages. Some things just aren't fair, but God knows and chose me for this path. Finding RNs with vent experience proved to be the biggest task. I grabbed the day shift and called the hours 8:00– 4:00, which was perfect for me and my son. It caused a bit of a flurry, as most nursing shifts are 7:00–3:00, 3:00–11:00, and 11:00–7:00. Surprisingly, they went along with it. Many nurses squawked. I won.

The anticipated day finally came, and the ambulance attendants brought Dr. M. into the house through the front door. He was smiling broadly. "Welcome home, Dr. M., welcome home." I had set up a table for the vent and made room for the monstrous oxygen tank. The transfer of equipment was made without difficulty, and Dr. M. was transferred to his new bed. He seemed very pleased with his location, which made me feel satisfied. I offered him a cup of tea, and he said yes—this was our first verbal communication. A representative from the nursing agency came by, as well as two of Dr. M.'s fellow neurologists.

I prayed, "I can do this, Lord. Please help me with every decision to keep this man safe until You call him home. Amen."

Next arrived an RN who would take over for me at the end of my shift. She said she was familiar with the vent. Why did I feel unsure? The next day, I arrived at 8:00 a.m. and met the overnight nurse. She said she did okay. It was then I decided to implement a shift diary for all the nurses to document what went on during their shift. Well, now, over the period of two weeks, Dr. M. fired nearly every nurse. The agency could not find any more nurses willing to come, as they didn't know the vent, oxygen, and suction on demand order. So on LPN wages, they sent me other RN and LPN nurses willing for me to teach, which I did. Eventually, we came up with a pretty solid team for round-the-clock care. Thank God. Consistency is very good for the team, but especially for Dr. M. Firing and hiring got to be a bit of a joke, however. If they looked sideways, they were gone! I finally had a talk with Dr. M. and told him I couldn't work every shift that was open, and he had to try and be more tolerant with the staff getting through the learning process. And he did!

Now came the first day I had to put Dr. M. on the commode using the Hoyer lift. This is a metal tri-stand of sorts that utilizes a canvas pad placed under the patient, hooked onto the lift, and then handcranked to lift the patient. It was on wheels, and carefully—very carefully and slowly—I moved the patient to the commode. The first time was a disaster. You see, as I was pushing him back into position over the hole, I stepped on his foot. Oh, my dear Lord. He hollered very loud—yelped, really—and then called me stupid. I completed the task at last, gave him his bell, and left the room, and I sobbed. I was sure he would fire me, but when I went back into the room after he rang his bell, he said nothing. I know he saw my reddened face. I had already profusely apologized to him when it happened. Nothing further was communicated. I successfully transferred him back to bed. This was the first of at least one thousand transfers to come. At the end of my shift, he said, "See you tomorrow." Guess I still had a job. Onward. The next hurdle was giving him a bed bath. I accomplished this task with numerous patients over the years. Here's a little side story. My first bed bath was in nursing training when I was told to prep the patient for inguinal surgery and a bath. Oh my, was he young and handsome! I asked him his name, and he said, "Father so-and-so." No, someone was having fun with me, and somehow, I finished shaving his private parts and bathing him, chatting nonstop to prevent myself from crying. I was eighteen at that time. When I left his room, there were four nurses standing outside, giggling like grade-schoolers.

Yes, there is a process. You start with the face and hands, upper body, and groin, which Dr. M. was able to do with his one hand. I swear he always skipped under his arms! Now, change the water. I finished his legs, then turned him onto his side and washed his back, etc. I could tell he was stressed, so I made conversation light. Eventually, I was told by other staff that he had a bad odor; I knew it, as he refused deodorant. Now comes the second talk.

"Dr. M., I am going to give you a complete bath today, and we are going to use deodorant because people are complaining about your BO."

Guess what he said? Absolutely nothing. He just laughed and laughed.

"Brits don't use deodorant," he later said.

"Well, they should."

Probably because of my precocious nature or nervousness about a full and very complete wash by me, I talked all the way through his bath. Nonetheless, we were starting to become friends.

I started grocery shopping and cooking for him. I know he appreciated home-cooked meals, and I didn't need any accolades. It was a nice way to take home dinner to my son too. It didn't take long for me to ascertain his likes and dislikes, and occasionally, he would request something, and I would do my best to make it. Salmon and mashed potato fried patties were his favorite. I said yuck; he said yum.

It was now approaching his sixty-fifth birthday, and since I had already met all his fellow neurologists and their spouses, who came to visit regularly, and his priest friend, who was the chaplain at the hospital, and others, I planned a surprise birthday party. I kept it simple with appetizers and a beautifully decorated cake with "Happy 65th Birthday, Dr. M." There was plenty of scotch, bourbon, and wine. I knew his friends quite well at this point, as they visited often. He was surprised and happy, chatty. Success. I took him into the family room for the party, and when he appeared tired, I returned him to his bed in the living room. The crowd then came into the living room, and I caught a nice picture of the group. Finally, I gently had to kick them out. He was exhausted, and so was I.

*Dr. Marsh's fellow neurologists and me and Dr. M in the center.
Happy sixty-fifth birthday!*

Life with Dr. M. became routine. He enjoyed being taken to the family room, where he would watch the birds from the feeder I had installed. This bird feeder had a metal pole, and he would laugh so hard at the tenacity of the squirrels climbing up or jumping from a nearby tree. Ah, the simple things in life. One day, I decided to grease the pole with Vaseline, as I couldn't keep up with the birdfeed. Well, we sat for over an hour watching the escapade unfold. We laughed and laughed until the vent started alarming because he wasn't getting enough air. What a brilliant memory, which we repeated often. Did you ever try to tell someone to stop laughing? Correct. Now we were howling like two crazy fools.

One seemingly ordinary day, I casually said to Dr. M., "Did you ever think about going back to England?" I'm telling you straight—if looks could kill, I would have been dead! Thank God it was the end of my shift and a Friday. I did not say goodbye that day, as I was hoping he would give it some thought and be willing to forgive me for my faux pas come Monday morning. Either that, or I would be fired. I was so fraught the entire weekend.

Monday did come, and I got the report from the night nurse saying he had been very quiet over the last two days. The nurse left, and Dr. M. rang his bell. *Here it is,* I thought.

I went in and said good morning, and he said, "When you're finished making my breakfast, come in—I want to speak to you." The time seemingly stopped at that moment. I felt shaky. I gave him his breakfast and departed to give him time to eat. A half hour or so later, he rang his bell, and I went in to face the music. He stated, "Were you serious when you said, 'Have I ever thought about going home to England?'"

I said, "Yes, I believe where there's a will, there's a way."

His response was, "Well, then, will you take me home to die?"

I said, "I will find a way!" We both cried, and I gave him a hug. Friendship solidified.

I had to get my children onboard.

There was no concrete plan yet. Heck, there was no plan at all! The first thing I thought I must do was to get Dr. M. off his dependency on the oxygen tank, as I knew he would never be able to fly. I told him as much, and he was willing to try short periods without the added oxygen. Eventually, he did very well, weaning down to two liters from four liters. I then decided to take him outside with a portable tank in the yard. He loved being outdoors looking at his flowers. He never lost his sense of smell or taste. Gradually, I would experiment with taking him to the end of the driveway and eventually a few houses away. It became longer and longer, as he kept saying, "I'm okay, go a little farther." Before you knew it, I was wheeling him all around the neighborhood. Oxygen was nearby if needed. This one day in particular, he made me stop to go through a pile of junk waiting for garbage pickup, and he insisted we take home a perfectly good old shovel (at least that was his observation). So here was this man with tubes for the vent across his chest in a hospital gown and a blanket over his knees (his preference) with a muddy rusty shovel across hislap. Dear God, but he was so delighted! I knew people were staring as they drove by us. I didn't care; he was happy and so was I.

Then came the day he was made to survive without the oxygen. We were two streets away, and suddenly the oxygen tank started making noises. I looked down at the gauge, and although it said 10 percent full, it was empty! I started to run toward home. He kept saying, "I'm fine," and was laughing. I was not laughing! As soon as we got to the house, I checked his oxygen saturation level, and it was within normal limits. A miracle had taken place, no doubt about it. No, I'm serious— he was determined to get there! Although the ravages of this dreadful disease robbed him of his muscle strength throughout his body, his mind was sharp as ever. The one thing ALS does not affect is the mind.

On a side note, Dr. M. was also a psychiatrist and a toxicologist. He traveled the world studying methyl mercury poisoning in pregnant women due to eating fish daily, as well as other environmental toxins. He repeatedly went to the Seychelle Islands, Japan, and north of Baghdad, Iraq, to complete his study. He was brilliant and had a great sense of humor. Quite a rare combination indeed. Laughter strengthened his lungs, as did God.

Yet one day sitting outside, I bravely stated, "I'm so sorry you have to go through this, Dr. M."

Without hesitation, he simply stated, "I'm not in any pain. I still have my faculties, and I can read the newspaper and visit with friends. All in all, it's not so bad." I will never forget his words of wisdom. Now he was also my mentor.

The next thing he did was purchase a Chrysler minivan, cash. Then he had an electric ramp installed on the passenger side so we could wheel him up the ramp and into the passenger seat to travel. Of course, we eliminated the passenger seat, and he stayed in his wheelchair. The second vent, which I insisted he purchase, was on the back of the wheelchair by this time.

Dr. M.'s home was put on the market, and passage was booked on the *Queen Elizabeth 2* passenger ship. He contracted a mover to pack and ship his furniture and clothing, leaving some clothes out for the cruise. I had them dry-cleaned and packed. He still favored his hospital gowns! I told him he couldn't go to the captain's dinner table in a gown. He agreed.

My daughter lived in the dorm at the university campus and was doing quite well. Although she wasn't happy about my going to another country, I assured her Dr. M. didn't have much longer to live, and I also needed this job. Little did I know. I left her in shock, still angry with me for leaving her dad and now leaving the country. I promised to call frequently and to write. My son was another matter. His biggest problem was leaving his beloved dog, MacGyver. We couldn't take him, as he would have to be quarantined for six months in England. This made no sense. My son was to start at the local school at home and then fly to England on his own one month later. I called Mr. X, and he had this habit of saying "FU" and hanging up. I began to think this was my middle name— Sue, FU. I had to write something up and have it documented and sent to him via my lawyer. He said no, my son said yes. The rules were endless. They included paying for all four round-trip flights: going initially, home for Christmas, home for Easter, and at the end of the school term in May. I agreed and signed his document. I could not possibly leave my son with his father.

It was then, one night, I went to the back porch of the house I had rented and began to cry and cry until I started to get down to pray on my knees. Suddenly, I found myself on my belly, flat out on the floor, calling out to God. I'm not sure how long I was there; my son was in bed. I kept asking, "God, if this is You putting this task in front of me— all of us, really—I ask please for Your blessing on this move and the safety and healing of my darling daughter's anger and emotions while I am away. Amen." The tears flowed. I felt assured somehow that He would be with us all. He was thus far.

I packed the rental house and put everything in storage except for the Christmas lights and decorations. My son was now going to spend a month with his father, and I worried. My son's passport came, and his flight was booked. (To be continued later.)

Dr. M. found a house with a private attached "granny flat," which is what it's called in the UK. Here, we call it an attached in-law space. He sold stock and purchased it.

Done. My space, I was told, had two bedrooms, a bathroom, a living room, and a small kitchen. Perfect.

The anticipated day finally came. The Chrysler minivan was packed solid, plus a car-top carrier full of necessities. The interior held one of his vents between the front seats, the suction machine, three people, and one in a wheelchair. Literally no place to wiggle. The commode and Hoyer lift went up top. Three suitcases for the trip aboard, plus additional belongings of mine and Debby's. Two of Dr. M.'s friends were at the ready to send us off. Of course, I knew they were aghast at the reality of it all. Debby drove us first, and I squeezed into a small space in the back seat and sat with her stuffed bear on my lap. We were waved off, and there was no turning back now. We left Rochester very early with an approximate eight-hour drive ahead assuming one to two stops going directly to the ship. We stopped only once and took turns going to the ladies' room; Dr. Marsh had his urinal. I suctioned.

We arrived literally just in time at the dock; they waited for us. When they brought a huge wagon toward the van, I was confused until I was told everything had to be removed to inspect for drugs, etc. We complied as quickly as possible, separating out the luggage, commode, wheelchair, and other necessities. The rest was put in storage aboard, including the van, once inspected. Finally, we were escorted to our room. I took the first twelve-hour shift. There was a twin bed separated from Dr. M.'s electric bed. I set up all the equipment and was ready to collapse. It was a beautiful suite with a huge picture window. Dr. M. was pleased.

The ship started to move, and Dr. M. asked to go to the main deck. I agreed, even as tired as I was. My coworker had already gone to her room. Debbie, one of the LPNs, made the decision to take the journey with us and then return immediately upon arrival in England on the Air France Concorde. By the time we got to the back of the ship's main deck, we were passing Lady Liberty. Dr. M. asked me to get him a cigarette. *What? People will arrest me,* I thought, looking at this dear man on a ventilator with all his tubes. I complied, as usual. Everyone was smoking, so it wasn't difficult to ask for one. I lit his cigarette and handed it to him. He mostly held it between his fingers as he waved goodbye to Ms. Liberty. We both cried tears of joy and sorrow. I finished the cigarette.

To be honest, I couldn't wait for my twelve-hour shift to be over. When my coworker came to the door, I said goodbye to Dr. M. and, "See you tonight." I headed down the hallway to my room when it occurred to me to have a dip in the Jacuzzi to relax my tired bones and catch my breath after a very long previous day and night. I must have thought I was Superwoman, but the way I was currently feeling said otherwise. In any case, I then retired to my room for some sleep, as I had one eye and one ear open all last night. I slept soundly.

When I awoke—now day two—I became aware of some movement in the ship. Ha, some movement became lots of movement. I showered and dressed to go get something to eat and was told in the restaurant that we were entering a full-force gale. A gale, for those of you who haven't traveled in the North Atlantic by ship, is what is otherwise known as a high-category hurricane. The date was September 29, 1995. I ate and then decided to check on Dr. M. He was doing fine, but my coworker was not. She looked dreadful and was experiencing motion sickness. She went back to her room, and I took over her remaining shift.

This was day two, and the weather was getting worse. The ship was really starting to rock more side to side with each passing minute. And then my stomach began to flip-flop, and I started to sweat profusely. Dear God, help! We called for the ship's doctor to come. In the meantime, I had to remove my top—leaving my bra on, of course— and apologize to Dr. M. What was he doing? He felt fine and was laughing! The nerve. I vomited two to three times before the ship's doctor arrived and said, "Follow me to the clinic down below deck." I had called my coworker, and she was not happy, but she came. I vomited again on the way down, and as soon as we arrived, I was given an injection to stop the seasickness. It took effect quickly—thank You, Lord— and I went back to Dr. M.'s room. Coworker left! Dr. M. told me to lie down on the bed. "Don't move, you'll be fine."

I was, and so was he. I think I passed out, and he never needed me or rang for me. End of day two. Three more days till we dock in Southampton.

Finally, it was time for my coworker to come back for the start of day three. I headed straight to the bar—yup, I did. The Jacuzzi was emptied, as it had been sloshing all its water over the entire deck. Only two other people plus the bartender were there. Rocking and rollin', we were. I think I ordered a vodka and tonic—no matter. I was sitting and chatting when, as in a horror movie, the ship turned completely over on its left, or port, side, and I found myself standing upright off the stool without any effort of my own. The bartender screamed, "Duck!" at the top of his lungs. No need to say again, and I tucked under the bar. Then I heard the noise of all the bottles crashing to the floor from off the shelves behind the bar, and I found myself holding on to the stool as the ship flipped to its right, or starboard, side. Eventually, we leveled out.

"Everyone okay?" someone asked. We were all shaken badly, but without cuts or bruises. The Titanic flashed into my mind briefly.

Of course, I raced to check on Dr. M. and my coworker, and they were both okay. Again, brief visions of his bed sliding out the picture window with him in it!

Day four, and the seas calmed. We had made it through the storm— thank God. We were all invited to the captain's table tonight for dinner. Of course, Dr. M. declined, and I couldn't blame him, but by God, we came this far—we should enjoy one nice meal. They graciously accommodated us in a private area in the upper-class dining room. It was gorgeous. Dr. M. looked wonderful, as I dressed him in a suit and white shirt and clipped on a bow tie to somewhat cover the trach tube. Now he was feeling like a father to me, not just a friend and mentor. I cut up his food and fed him, and the food was more than delicious. Cheese platters followed by dessert trays completed the meal. We were fairly inconspicuous, despite the *pish-put, pish-put* sounds of the ventilator. The captain did come to pay his respects, and it was lovely. End of day four—a success.

The morning of day five came too soon. I got everything packed and ready to go. My coworker assisted in getting Dr. M. by Hoyer lift back into his wheelchair. He was ready, and we three made it! Hallelujah! Passports in hand, we were escorted ahead of others down to customs and then to our Chrysler Buick minivan. Again, another daunting task—repacking the entire van! We had to do it quickly, trying to remember how we did it in the first place. Oh, I might as well mention that it was pouring rain. Coworker Debby wanted to go directly to the airplane home, and who could blame her? I convinced her to stay just three more days, and she said okay.

I drove out of Southampton Pier into five o'clock traffic in the rain. Slow and steady on the wrong side of the road! I acclimated somewhat when I approached our first roundabout, going left, with three lanes of traffic. *I'm going to die,* was my first thought.

Dr. M. calmly said, "Carry on," which I later learned meant go halfway around and then go straight. Horns were honking from all sides. When I eventually carried on, Dr. M. was laughing so hard it set all the alarms off, and he had tears running down his cheeks. He said, "I never thought I'd get all the way back home to die in a roundabout!"

After that, the drive was uneventful and took us approximately three hours to arrive at Villa Mouette, Canford Cliffs, Poole. This small village lies two miles between Bournemouth and Poole Harbor. Dr. M.'s brother, also a physician, was there waiting for us. The furniture had not arrived and was somewhere in the Atlantic, presumably. I got Dr. M. in bed, only to discover that this was not an electric bed. No way! Yes, way! There was a single bed in my room, one in my son's room—no sheets, no pillow—and another bed upstairs. Period.

However, the worst problem became apparent when I was told the so-called nurses were basic aides and could not operate the vent or handle any other duties that would be required. That, I'm happy to say, was HIS job. I had no choice but to put Dr. M. in the hospital the following morning, as I was more than spent and slept in a chair next to his bed. His brother left, saying he knew nothing about the ventilator, and I was on my own. Thank you, kind sir.

I went with Dr. M. to Poole Hospital in the morning and instructed the nurses and doctors. They were excellent. Afterward, I went back to the house and caught my breath, if only momentarily. He was there for five days and raved about the English food and the good care he received. In the meantime, I got my coworker to agree to stay for three months. I will now call her Debby, and I thanked God for her every day. She was such a good help and kept me sane and laughing.

Debby and David
Thanksgiving in England, 1995

My first task today was to hire a nursing agency. They are called sisters here in England. They balked loudly, stating, "Oh dear, we don't do vents here in England." (Truly a survival-of-the-fittest mindset.)

I felt like saying, "Well, you do now," but instead I said, "I am willing to teach if they are willing to learn." Eventually, when they found out he was a neurologist from America and his brother was a GP here in Poole, they acquiesced and said they would give it a go. Lord, please help us once again. And of course, He did.

On day two in my new environment, I assessed what had to be done next. I had to figure out how to drive on my own without knowing where anything was—shopping, etc. I had no neighbor to ask, no GPS in those days, and no map. So I ventured out very slowly, went about a mile, and saw a sign for a home store. I went around the roundabout and came right home. That was enough for now. My room was nicely painted; my son's room was not.

1. Purchase paint and brushes, sheets, and pillows.

2. No closets; ask where to find a couple for clothes. A niece of Dr. M.'s stopped in and gave me help to find a "charity shop"that had used furniture, including a dresser for me and a smalltable for my son's homework.

3. There was a couch in the living room, a small table with two chairs, and a TV.

4. The kitchen just had a counter and a tiny refrigerator—period.

5. The bathroom was a bathroom with a long, skinny tub and had a small shelf above the commode for toiletries. To flush, you pull a chain suspended from the ceiling. One small addition: drain spiders the size of a hardball, with a body as big as a dime. Charming.

On day two, I pulled up my big girl panties and ventured out. After I purchased some white paint and a brush, I asked questions and was told how to get to the charity shop. Almost everything I needed was right there. I bought two wardrobes, a clothes dresser, a chair, and a small table for my son's homework. The people were so kind and offered to bring everything to the house that afternoon. They instructed me where to go for new but lower-quality bedding. Perhaps tomorrow.

Back home, I received a call from the brother to tell me Dr. M.'s furniture would be arriving in the morning, and he would come over. With that news, I decided to paint my son's room. I skipped the ceiling, as it was ten feet high and there was no ladder, and then I waited for the movers. Everything fit in perfectly! I unpacked my clothes and put them in the new wardrobe and dresser, which had a good-sized mirror. It was starting to feel like home. The linens and drapes would have to come another day.

Debby and I went out tonight to the Haven Hotel, which sits on the English Channel. If we walked out the front door and turned left, then went down a steep hill, there was Poole Harbor, which I am told is the largest natural harbor in the world, second to Sydney, Australia. If we walked ten feet from the side of the house, better known as a bungalow, there was a steep incline, known as a chine, which was tree-lined on both sides and took us directly down to the beach. This was the English Channel. Our eyes could barely take it all in. The beauty was almost beyond description. This beach was rated the number one best beach in all of the UK. Spectacular views in all directions. Beach huts dotted the promenade (a cement walkway all along a five-mile stretch between the beach and the huts), and they were used year-round by the hardy Brits to sit after a swim and make their tea. I'm talking about January and February months too! Elderly women with their white plastic bathing caps on.

The next day, the movers arrived with Dr. M.'s furniture. I already had it rearranged in my mind where things should go—of course I did. The electric hospital bed was going into the living room, facing the fireplace, and the couch, I thought, would look nice on a slant to the right of the fireplace and within earshot of the bed so that visitors could chat easily with Dr. M. The chair could fit almost anywhere. The bed Dr. M.'s brother had put in his original room went out the door. The dining room table and six chairs fit nicely in the dining area, which had a pass-through from the kitchen. This is where the nurses would sit with a monitor to listen to the sounds of the vent and any disturbances when they were not in Dr. M.'s room. The electric wheelchair and the backup vent went under the stairs.

Take note—to be continued later. All the worry and concern about the delivery turned into an easy transfer into the new home. All the remaining additional belongings went upstairs in one of the two bedrooms. Debby, as I said, resided in the second bedroom upstairs, where she could crank up her music. I seem to remember George Michael singing "Faith" as a particular favorite of hers at the time. Indeed, you do! The house construction was built with solid cement walls with plaster over the top—not at all like our wood construction and plywood here in the States. I never heard anything until I entered her room. Later on, I had the opportunity to observe the new construction of another building. No wonder these buildings in England last forever, which they do.

The following day was Dr. M.'s day. He came home from the hospital, and once again, I was ready. He had so many stories to tell us. Mostly, it was about the food he ate and the wonderful tea. Not much about his care, although when I turned him onto his side, I became aware that he was not turned very often. I always had a strict rule—strict, bossy woman that I apparently am. He was to be turned every two hours, no excuses, no refusal on his part either. He admitted they did not turn him ever during his stay! There weren't any open sores, but he was very red and close to breaking down. He received many back and buttock massages that first week.

The nurses started to arrive, one by one, and were trained. Some stayed, and some flew out the front door almost as soon as they arrived. The good ones stayed, and before long, there was a great group of staff. They were trained in the vent, suctioning, sterile technique, and other necessary components of taking care of Dr. M. I was responsible for keeping track of their hours and schedules.

I also kept track of my own and was paid separately in pounds, not US dollars. It was a meager hourly wage, but with all the other perks, I could not possibly complain.

It came fairly quickly, adjusting to the village. Where to buy dry goods (the grocer), where to buy meat (the butcher), where to buy vegetables (the greengrocer), where to buy bread and pastries (of course, the bakery—I had a difficult time staying away from there!) and the pharmacist (called the chemist in the UK) for medications. There was also a post office, which, in addition to sending mail, had a large array of greeting cards and candies. A local bank, where I had to open an account to deposit or cash my checks, was one of my first stops. Oh yes, there was a car dealership— and the best place of all—the travel agencies. But that part is another story altogether. I introduced myself to the village and was now known as Ms. Nurse Sue. Lovely tiny village of Canford Cliffs. One short street with establishments on either side. Simply lovely.

Upon meeting the current doctor in charge (who also did not know anything about ventilators!), frankly, he was stunned looking at Dr. M. lying there quite happy and chatty on this machine which, once again, would never be allowed in England. "He has a fatal disease, you know," he remarked. I never called him except once to obtain a urine sample for a possible UTI. He was required to make house calls—all GPs (general practitioners) did. This was the second time I was told I was on my own, unless I wanted to contact someone in London. Sure, I'll call when I need someone to drive for three hours to figure out why the vent isn't working. I was very strict with visitors, including his family, making it very clear that a "simple cold" could cost Dr. M. his life.

Figuring out the 2' x 3' icebox, which we call a refrigerator, was another adjustment. But the real tester was leaving the eggs on the counter. You purchased them off the shelf, unrefrigerated, from the food market. Interesting. I adapted to these new rules. A very silent dairy truck, more like a large golf cart with a box on the back, was my favorite surprise. The same gentleman would come twice a week to deliver the glass jar milk bottles, and when they were empty and washed, I put them back onto the stoop. Dr. M. loved the milk with the cream on top and ordered two bottles each delivery. Unbeknownst to me, I found out the bluebirds, a magpie, loved the cream and came and pecked the paper top and drank the inch or so of cream off the top of the bottle, then happily flew away. The first time I went out to get the bottles, I did not hear the delivery and I discovered the cream theft. I told Dr. M., and he laughed and laughed as it brought back fond memories. I was quick to get the bottles off the front stoop after that!

As quick as a wink, it was time for my son to arrive. His room was ready. So I went by bus to London—three hours, but I think you know that. I was on time for his arrival. He never got off the plane! Where, what, how—sputter, cry. I quickly took aside one of the attendants from the flight, and she said, "Oh, I'm sorry, he didn't get on our flight." Then where was my child, who was supposed to be escorted safely to me? I was sent to the American Airlines office. It was there they informed me of a snowstorm in Chicago that had grounded them there, and a stewardess had accompanied him to the hotel room which they shared. I was told he was well cared for and would arrive tomorrow. Okay, three hours back on the bus. One would think his father would have called.

The next day came, and I trusted God. This time, I took a cab, and I was told my son was in customs being questioned. After nearly two hours, I was allowed to go back and see him. What had he done, and where was the problem? I had always told my son to never lie to me because if he needed my help, I would need to know the truth, the whole truth. Well, it seems when they asked him how long he was staying and where, he blurted out, "Oh, I'm going to live with my mom and Dr. M., and um, oh, I'm going to school here this year." Well, the plan was simple: "I'm here to visit my mom" clearly did not work. Although it wasn't a lie, it wasn't the full truth either. My fault. Then they wanted to speak to me before he would be released. I told them about Dr. M., etc.; and without another word, they made an appointment for us to go to customs down in Poole after two weeks.

God bless the taxi driver for staying. We were both exhausted, and my son was not happy. He didn't care where we were going. "Just get there, Mom." Three hours later, we were back at our new home. I had the taxi driver go past the sea, but my son didn't care at this point about anything but sleep. He said hello to Dr. M., and then I showed him his room—more like a large closet. He flopped on his bed and slept for fifteen hours.

I made him something to eat when he woke. He was a bit bewildered. I purposely didn't schedule myself to work that day, and after he ate, I drove him around to see the beautiful harbor and the English Channel. He was impressed and asked a thousand questions. The next surprise was getting him a used bike that I bought with my first paycheck. Immediately, he wanted to take a ride. So I hopped on my bike, and he on his, and away we went down the chine and onto the promenade all the way to Bournemouth and back. By the time we got back, jet lag kicked in for him, and he ate and went right back to bed.

I had already made a visit to Uplands International, his new school, and spoke to the headmaster and his new teacher. I was told he would be moved ahead one grade to coincide with his age. Further, he would be taking second-year French, first-year Latin, world history, sailing, along with science, English, and math. I was freaking out, and so was he! Nonetheless, we forged ahead.

I hired a French au pair to bring him up to speed, and she never once spoke English to him. She introduced herself, and because she was young and beautiful, he responded well to her. She even taught him how to pronounce his name. Off to the races! She took him everywhere, and it was a brilliant way to teach him the basics of French. She also took him to a French restaurant and made him orderoff the menu. He's a smart kid, and within just a few weeks, he was upto speed with his class.

All in all, life went smoothly, and he was adapting without medication to his eight classmates—five girls and three boys. He rode his bike to school and back every day, past the golf course and the Oriental Gardens. Yes, there were glitches along the way. He liked to stay after class on Wednesdays to feed the python live frogs.

Once, he said to me in a total British accent, "Mum, may I go to Alan's for tea after school tomorrow?"

Who was this person speaking? Of course, I said, "You may." Tea is around 5:00 p.m. and is like a light supper.

Round about 6:00 p.m., he came back home, walked in calmly, and said, "Don't freak out. I fell over the handlebars on the golf course because I forgot the brakes are opposite on this bike!" His face—his gorgeous face—his nose and chin were in bad shape but, by this time, were not bleeding and had scabbed over somewhat. His friend's mum had taken care of him and then brought him home. He later admitted he was going too fast, tried to brake, hit a rise, and flew into the air over the handlebars, landing on his face. Lesson learned?

He refused to go to school for three days. I called his schoolteacher and explained he didn't want to ride his bike to school and didn't want me to take him. Not that I could; I was taking care of Dr. M. and couldn't just say, "Gee, could you take care of yourself for a while so I can take my son to school?"

The teacher said, "Mrs. Cuminale, don't say another word about it to him. One day, he will get up, get dressed, hop on his bike, and come to school. He will then have to make up the work." Sure enough, on day three, he was up early, showered, and put on his uniform—navy blue sport coat, white dress shirt, tie, beige slacks, and specific socks and shoes. Indeed, he looked smart. There was a second incident involving a bus bumping the rear of his bike so that he had to pull over and fell off. I think he is learning the buses have the right of way here; no messing around. Those are only two of the stories I know about.

Christmas holiday came all too quickly that year. It seemed my son had just gotten settled, gotten to know his classmates, and gotten into a good routine, and now I had to fly him back to Rochester, New York, because I had signed that document! By now, I was driving everywhere without any difficulties, so I drove him to London's Heathrow Airport for his flight and saw him off with a stewardess caretaker. My son, now thinking he was a world traveler, didn't see why he needed a caretaker. "Because rules are rules, son."

I had preplanned to take an adventure to Ireland for three days with my friend Barbara. We met at a club called David Lloyds—not a club per se, but a workout, exercise, private pool club. It had three restaurants. One was of five-star quality and expensive—I ate there twice; quite fancy. The second one was more pub-style, and you could go there in your workout clothes, all smelly and sweaty—so civilized. I went there only once and thought I had been kidnapped. It was full to the brim of sweaty male Brits watching the World Cup soccer match. Insanity comes to mind. Third restaurant was perfect.

Might I mention "the troubles" between Northern Ireland and England at the time we were there? Well, Mary Susan wanted to visit Northern Ireland to see where her grandmother was born, don' tya know?. I had been working on getting my Irish citizenship, thanks to Dr. M., who had told me I could get the papers at the Irish Consulate Office in London since both my grandparents came from Ireland—Grandma Heslop from the north, and Grandpa Flanagan from County Mayo in the south. But that's another story.

So without telling Dr. M., off we went to Dublin from Bournemouth Airport direct. This tiny plane held six passengers. I thought I might have to pedal to get it off the ground. Nonetheless, off we went, up and down in seventeen minutes. I rented a car, but Barbara refused to sign up as a driver. She, being English, was only going to satisfy her friend. Well, now we were on our way. Stick shift, me sitting on the right side of the tiny car, and, of course, I wanted a cigarette. I asked Barbara to light one for me. She didn't smoke, but I begged her, and she did—it looked so funny, trying to puff to get it lit. Then, she handed me the cigarette, and, being left-handed, I couldn't figure out how to flick the ashes out the right window with my left hand! I tried to get the window down. We couldn't stop laughing as I handed the cigarette back to her to dispose of.

How did the accident happen? said the officer. *Poor girls, had to have a smokey. Thank God no accident ever happened.*

Well, we got to the border between the north and south just at dusk, and the armed guards would not let us cross. They told us to stay at a bed and breakfast and come back in the morning. We had no choice. As it happened, there was a sign directing us to a charming place just a mile away on the bay of the Irish Sea. The sweet caretaker said, "I only have one room with a double bed," and we said, "Fine, we'll take it." She made us a light snack and then escorted us to the tiny room with a view. I heard some young men singing and starting a bonfire on the beach. *How sweet,* I thought, and drifted off to sleep. Neither Barbara nor I heard a thing in the night, but come morning, there was a pounding on our door. Startled, I opened it to the caretaker, and she had this look of panic on her face when she said, "Are you okay?"

"Yes," I assured her, "we slept soundly."

She said, "Oh dears, they burned three buildings down!" Well, three buildings were half the tiny street! With that, we dressed and flew out the door, never looking back.

Back at the border, we were asked a couple of questions and allowed to cross into Northern Ireland. We didn't drive more than two miles when, from out of the bushes on either side of the road, popped up six soldiers in uniforms with rifles pointed right at the car. One of them shouted, "Stop!" Naturally, I stopped, and he approached my window and asked, "Where are you from?"

I said, "America."

"Why are you here?"

"I want to see where my grandmother was born."

It was Barbara's turn. "And you?"

"I'm from England," as if to say, *I don't like you, and don't mess with me, kid.*

I then saw the soldier point for the rifles to be lowered. *Phew.* I then flirted with him a bit—he was ever so cute—

asking where we could get some breakfast, and he pointed out the way. Onward we went.

After getting something to eat, we went to the area of my grandmother's birth and found the schoolhouse I believe she went to. The graveyard was across the street, and I took a few pictures, thinking some may be relatives. We came alongside an elderly gentleman with a cane and asked him for directions, which he gladly gave. "Down here a bit, turn left down the one lane, go a bit, turn right, you'll find it."

"Thank you, kind sir." We followed his instructions, and guess what —we ended up right back at the old gentleman! It was then we discovered the man was blind! I'm sorry, but as we drove away (and I could hardly drive), the two of us were laughing and crying like two children, not adults.

We tried again on our own and got behind a man walking his two horses back to his house. He turned around to see who we were, and I stopped and got out of the car.

I introduced myself, explained our situation, and he said, "Oh, you must come up to the house and have tea with me and my wife." I would have followed him anywhere; he was even more handsome than the soldier! So follow him and his horses we did. He went in and spoke to his wife, and out she flew to give me a hug!

"The kettle's on. Come sit. We'll have tea on the lawn." The three children set out a blanket on the lawn and jumped around us like we came from outer space. One was cuter than the next. They asked me a million questions, which I was happy to answer. They sang us a couple of songs, and I thought I would cry. A memory for life. I snapped a couple of pictures. This made up for the prior troubles, and I've decided I love Ireland.

We kept on driving north for a short while and then took the road west and south, crossed the border without fanfare, and headed toward Kiltimagh, County Mayo. When we pulled into the tiny town, everyone was dancing and drinking in the middle of the street. "Here we go," was my first thought. We found the hotel and settled into our room. The innkeeper told us they were still partying after a wedding. We couldn't have cared less, but we were too tired and fell fast asleep. End of day two.

Day three took us to the only bar in town to meet the town historian. A nicer man you will never meet. He loved his job and knew all about the Flannigans who lived in house number 7 just across the road and down a bit. Then he directed us to the local Catholic church for more information. The priest was a bit frustrated but led us to the proper book of marriages and baptisms, then said we had to be quick because he had to leave. I wrote as fast as the pen would go, notingnames and dates, and then we left. I noted the graveyard, but as far as I knew, all my relatives had moved to America in the early 1900s. We had a long drive ahead of us back to Dublin, where we booked into a lovely hotel. We had time to walk the main street, do a wee bit of shopping, and have a nice dinner. Wonderful bed, breakfast, and off to the Dublin Airport we went. This time, it was a four-passenger plane with props, and I sat directly behind the pilot. Of course, I flirted.

My son was gone for eight days before I had to drive to London again to pick him up from the airport. I wish I could say he was happy to be back—well, not at least for the first couple of days. He had left his father crying, and that disturbed him greatly. Before long, it was January, and sailing lessons were to begin in Poole Harbor. He perked up with that news, along with being chosen to feed the python his frogs on Wednesdays. Currently, all was well.

It wasn't long before I had met Dr. M.'s entire family. In fact, their visits had already begun to dwindle. There was Dr. M.'s brother and his wife, plus their seven children, five spouses, and a few grandchildren.

I started to amass a few friends over time, each one unique and varying in age. One fine Sunday, I got them all to come to the beach by Jazzy's Café. The youngest was eighteen—legal in England—and he always brought booze and cups to share. A lorry driver, who used to transport goods throughout Europe, would always join us when he was back in town. He brought his "smokies." Then there was Josie. She was, the oldest at the time, who brought tea and cookies. Another great friend, who owned a green grocer, brought a veggie tray. I brought a blanket and cheese and crackers. Of course, my dearest friend Barbara was always available on Sundays. She usually brought sweet treats. Somehow, there was always room on that blanket for us all, ranging in age from eighteen to seventy-two, and nobody cared about the differences. We were always laughing and enjoying the beautiful English Channel, the sailboats, the motorboats, each other, and the sunshine. Most people think England is always cloudy and dark like the old British black-and-white movies. Not so—not even close. The sea water keeps the air warm enough inland about two miles so that palm trees and similar fauna are dotted all along the shoreline. Who knew? We continued this nearly every week unless I as off on some three-day weekend.

Debbie stayed about three months before she went back to the states. Although we had great adventures, we lost touch after the new year.

My friend Barbara took me all over England and France. The first time we went to Nice, France, there were four of us. Because I was accustomed to driving on the right side of the road in America—like they do in France—I was elected to be the designated driver. That was a real flip of the switch in my mind. We rented a car, if you could call it that. It barely fit the four of us inside, let alone four suitcases, purses, and beach bags. Everyone had one or two things on their laps for the trip to our beachside villa. That would have been a phenomenal photo—more than likely illegal, as I could not see out of any window or the rearview mirror. Thanks, girls. Oh, what a time we had putting on the Ritz in the best of hotels. I could write a book about this trip alone. Marvelous, darlings, simply marvelous.

It was approaching Easter holiday, time to take my son back to Heathrow for yet another trip to Rochester. I took Barbara with me this time, and after getting my son safely on his flight, we went to Chelsea, where her daughter lives with two guys, just sharing the rent. One gentleman was a concert pianist and played for me on his baby grand. I was mesmerized. Barbara's daughter did the draperies for one of the museums and designed her own fabric. Barbara was in real estate and did quite well. We did some shopping in Chelsea—very upscale and unaffordable for little ole me, but I looked! We were taken to a great restaurant for a lively meal with good company. I had to get back to Dr. M., so we left very early the next morning for the three-hour trip back.

Easter weekend came, and Barbara said, "Get some time off, we're going to Paris for the weekend on the train." The nurses always covered my hours for me, and when there were bank holidays, I would do a twenty-four-hour shift for them. She set the whole thing up. Back to her daughter's in Chelsea, then the train the next morning direct to Paris through the Chunnel between Dover and France. We decided to have a cocktail in the bar, standing, going 90 mph on the fast train. Good Friday, and I visited the most beautiful city in the world. Barbara took me to the Eiffel Tower, and yes, I went all the way to the top. The last bit you had to walk up, and of course, I did. The views were indescribable. The next day, we went to Notre-Dame Cathedral, as we instinctively knew we could never get in on Easter Sunday. There are no words to describe the beauty of the interior, the smells, the sounds, and the reverent spiritual feeling that came over me. There was only one tiny problem—my stomach was doing flip-flops. You see, we had dined at a restaurant the night before, and I decided to have escargot. I ate all eight of them with champagne. No need to give details—use your imagination. We had already checked out of the hotel, but we went back and asked if we could stay awhile. Seeing I looked green, the gentleman graciously let us back into the room, which had not yet been cleaned. Things progressed, let's just say, and we left by taxi for the train and home.

My son came back from his Easter vacation in Rochester and was again disturbed and sad. That is, until I told him I wanted to give him a fourteenth birthday party at the beach with all his classmates. Dangle the carrot? I kept it simple—sandwiches, fruit, drinks, and of course, cake. I believe they all had fun, as did my son. Middle school hormones in full gear. As Uplands was an international school, his friends came from varied family backgrounds and ethnicities, which was an education all by itself. There was only one month left to the school term, and then he would be back in the States with his father until I returned.

I surprised my son with a trip to Normandy, France, on a motorcoach. It was a day trip, which I told him about the night before, as we had to be at the coach at 6:00 a.m. He didn't seem very enthused until we pulled into the Chunnel and were able to get out of the coach and stretch. It was then that he found it cool that we were under the water—the English Channel—and were some of the first to do so. The bell sounded for us to get back on board, and whoosh, we were back on land in France. The coach drove the entire coastline of Normandy, and he took numerous photos of the land where so many of our soldiers died on the beaches here. We were both quiet, staring at the land with the sea looking so peaceful. Not long after, we arrived in Le Havre and left the coach for a walk and to find a restaurant. I wanted to take him to a French place and hear him order in French. No go. He wanted something from the convenience shop—chips, a Coke, and a sandwich. I went along as usual. All he wanted to do was walk the pier and see the fish and boats, which we did. He was tired and admitted he had not slept much. Understandable, son, but I hope you remember this trip when you are older. He slept most of the way home.

Finals came, and he did very well indeed. In fact, he got accommodations from the headmaster of Uplands. Well done, son, well done indeed.

My son is now back in the USA, and I was without my two children for the first time in sixteen years. Dr. M. was doing quite well, although he was losing his ability to turn the pages of his newspaper. The nurses and I assisted him. It was a hard blow for him. The family visits became fewer and fewer. My heart was breaking for him. He was happy that the local parish vicar came at least once a week for a visit. He also loved hearing about the nurses' families and their lives.

The summer, now free from parental duties, was a new experience. I thanked God for my new friends who kept me going, and they were fond of Dr. M. I took a great photo of our group during one of their visits. He was very gracious to my motley crew.

Mary, Aaron, Rose, Dr. Ken, Steve,
Barbara, Ellie, Sheena, Jose, Fred

One beautiful day, I suggested to Dr. M. that we go for an outing to the New Forest. The New Forest National Park is a local government district in Hampshire, England. It is noted for its wandering free ponies, deer, cattle, and the like. Around 90 percent of the forest is owned by the Crown and has been managed since 1923. It was formally designated by William the Conqueror in 1079, so it's now about 1,000 years old. The wild ponies average around 5,000, and they always have the right of way. If they decide to lie down in the middle of the road, you must either wait or turn around. Absolutely no horn honking or you will be fined!

Off we went on our adventure together. He directed our path, and when we were well within the forest, he said, "Suction," so I pulled into a car park. I went into my normal routine—putting on gloves, turning on the machine, all while noticing a pony in my peripheral vision. He was coming closer and closer to the car. Dr. M. said, "Why don't you go and pick some blackberries just over there first? I'm okay." So ever dutiful, I obliged, picked a large handful, and brought them back, setting them in his lap. I cleaned my hands, donned the gloves again, and suctioned him. Now the pony was upon us! I jumped into the driver's seat just in time to see the pony's head eating the berries off Dr. M.'s lap. He found the strength to raise his hand and pet the pony, with a look on his face like a ten-year-old beaming with the biggest smile. I swear he told everyone that story for weeks after. A brilliant memory indeed.

I got Dr. M. down to the beach often. There were many well-known, designated areas of the beachfront—family beach, singles beach, gay beach, nude beach, dog beach. Something for everyone. There were no signs; you just got the vibe. Dr. M. loved the beach nearest us, where it was the norm for women to take off their bathing suit tops. I never did, but once my friends stole my top while I was lying on my stomach and kept saying, "Prude, prude, prude." Finally, after thirty minutes, I sat up, and they gave me back my suit! I thought the British were supposed to be the proper ones.

The summer flew by quickly, and now it was September. My son would be starting high school, and my daughter her second year of university. Hard to believe. I prayed for them often, and my phone bill was astronomical.

My friend Barbara said, "I'm taking you somewhere special for your fiftieth birthday." My only instructions were: It's in London, and dress like you are going to a wedding. Okay. She drove. I bought a beautiful black pencil skirt and a Kelly-green jacket with a fabulous widebrimmed hat. I felt smart. Still not knowing the surprise, she pulled up to the side entrance of the Ritz. We were greeted by the fully dressed British formal-wear attendant, who opened my door and said, "Welcome, miss." What? She was treating me to high tea at the Ritz!

We were escorted to the tearoom, and Barbara was in her element. She was in control of the ordering and such, and I let her. Tea, cucumber sandwiches, scones, fruits, and, of course, fresh clotted cream. Clotted cream is only made in Cornwall, the westernmost area of England. For those unfamiliar with this delectable substance, it's like a thick, spreadable whipped cream, naturally sweet and so delicious on a scone with strawberry jam. Then I spotted them—going past to another table—champagne flutes. I want some! Barbara relinquished control over to me, and I ordered; after all, it was my birthday.

On the way out, I was curious and a bit tipsy, and I told Barbara I just wanted to check the prices of the rooms. Her pat answer on so many outings was, "Oh, Susan, you can't do that!" Well, I did, and I booked their last double room—on me! We had no luggage and didn't care. After a quick check of the room, gilded with gold on the ceiling, unbelievably scented soaps and amenities, what caught my eye was a bowl full of fruit. I thought the plums were fake, but I picked one up and no—they were real plums, egg-washed and fine sugar-coated, placed just so in a silver bowl. Yes, I had one right then, and it tasted like it had just been picked from a summer-ripened tree. I thought I was in hotel heaven. I booked us for dinner in the ballroom, and we made our way downstairs, with Barbara pointing out celebrities whom I had no idea about, but she was impressed.

As we walked into the ballroom and were seated, we noticed that the two of us and only one other table of two males were not a couple. Well, I couldn't be sure of the two males. The fifteen-piece orchestra began to play soft music, and I placed my hand under the white tablecloth, touched Barbara's leg, and said, "Oh, darling, you are so special to me." She and I cracked up laughing as politely as we could. The five-course dinner was as beautiful and delicious as any I've ever had. Thank you, Barbara, for a fabulous birthday memory. After dinner, we went to a nearby club and watched the dancing until we were asked to join. We danced the night away until 5:00 a.m. When they closed the underground dancehall, we went back to our room, though we were asked to go out with the group to breakfast. Barbara was tired—ha ha—I was exhausted. Checkout was at 11:00 a.m., and we slowly made our way to the entrance to collect our car. The doors were opened, we shared a few laughs with the doorman, and we snapped a photo. Back home to Canford Cliffs, giggling along the way. When I returned to Dr. M.'s, there was a surprise waiting for me—fifty, that's right, *fifty* long-stemmed red roses. But that's another story.

It was about this time that my mind started to turn toward Rochester and my two children. I hadn't seen my daughter in a year. As much as I missed her, I was in a dilemma. So I discussed with Dr. M. the idea of putting an advertisement in the newspapers for an additional nurse, one that could take my place in an emergency and stay at the house 24-7. He agreed. About three days went by when I received a call regarding the ad. The woman introduced herself as Betty and proceeded to tell me about a gentleman from Istanbul, Turkey, who was a doctor there and was staying at her home. He was studying English at the University of Bournemouth. I listened and then said, "Thank you for his interest. Could he come by for an interview?" I knew Dr. M. wouldn't be happy, as he didn't want a male nurse. She said yes, and I asked for his name. Surely, his name is Ufuk!

And she pronounced it, "You Fuck?" Brits have this way of asking a question at the end of every sentence.

Instantly, I said, "Barbara, you got me," and started to laugh.

Betty said, "No dear, my name is Betty." I was now laughing harder until she said, "Excuse me, dear, are you well?"

I calmed myself and asked her to spell it for me.

"Yes, dear, U-F-U-K."

"And his last name please?"

"Yildirim—Y-I-L-D-I-R-I-M."

The time to meet was set for 3:00 p.m. the next day.

Dr. M. was listening to my conversation from his living room and rang his bell. I went in, and he wanted to know what was so funny, so I told him the story. He said, "No, not me, not lately."

I replied, "No, me either," and we both got into a riotous laugh. Rose, the Irish nurse from County Cork, came in for her shift, and we told her about Ufuk coming tomorrow. She joined in the laughter.

The next day was upon us. I was not planning to introduce our new doctor by name, so I deliberately made it for 3:00 p.m. Rose had gone home the night before and told her husband, Arom, the story. His reply was, "Why do you think this name is so funny? I have a good friend in Baghdad whose name is Morefuk!"

Little darling 4'10" Rose came in a few minutes early and told us what Arom had said. Need I tell you? All the bells, pips, and peeps were alarming because Dr. M. couldn't catch his breath from laughing so hard—tears-in-the-eyes laughter. But not now—the doorbell rang. It was 3:00 p.m. I calmed myself, went to the French doors, and opened them. "Do come in" was all I could muster. "I'm Susan, the head nurse." I escorted them into the front room, shut the door, and ran back to my room—coward.

Side note: Three years later, I was invited to visit Istanbul by Ufuk. During that two-week trip traveling throughout Turkey, his friends kept calling him "Ooh Fook," with long Os. Oh, those Brits and their phonetic English! He thought that was the proper pronunciation, not having learned the slang term yet. Silly me. Also, just by the way, I returned home safely through Newark Airport the evening of September 10, 2001. Thank you, Lord!

Dr. M. liked Ufuk, despite him being male. Ufuk was also a doctor and was willing for me to teach him the ventilator, suctioning, and all the other pertinent information. He was hired.

The next time he came, I walked him into the village to meet the chemist, greengrocer, and all the other people in town. I introduced him as Doc. He didn't ask why. Thank you, Lord.

He picked things up quickly and settled into his new home upstairs, where Debby once lived. I was so happy to have him, and I booked a trip home in late September. Ufuk was ready, plus all the other nurses were there to help. Five days was all I could afford to be away. It was a good visit with my son, daughter, and parents. I blinked, and it was time to return.

All was well when I came back. Ufuk took a break for one week to complete his exams.

One normal day shift, I was in the kitchen when suddenly, I didn't hear the *pish-put* noise of the vent. I ran into his room as he was ringing his bell. The vent had stopped—no warning—just stopped. I hand-bagged Dr. M. for a couple of minutes, and he indicated he was okay. I said, "Dr. M., I must go and get the other vent from the back of your motorized wheelchair. Are you ready?" He nodded yes. I bagged him again, ran to the cubby under the stairs, and tried to maneuver the chair by hand, but it wasn't working. Drastic times call for drastic measures—I picked up the entire vent and ran back to his room, bagged him again while plugging it in, and transferred the tubing. I bagged him again, turned on the machine, and it worked immediately. I stood there and watched him slowly return to normal breathing and color. When he was settled, he said, "Well, I think we're due a scotch!" Always on the bright side—that was Dr. M. He could have died, but God had other plans. The next day, he purchased a British vent. I was very glad Ufuk wasn't there for this incident.

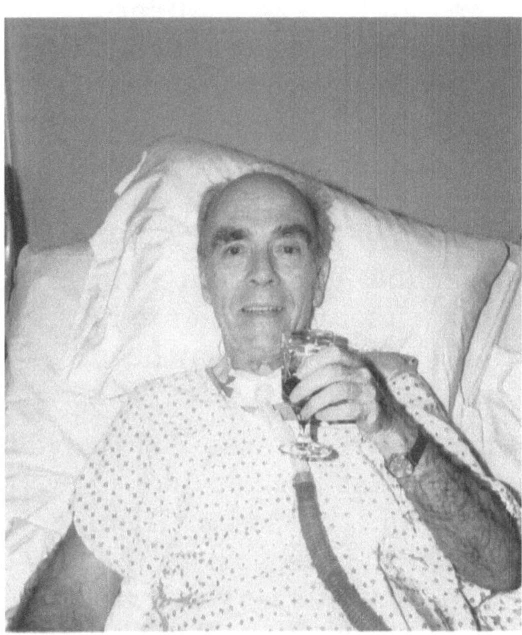

After my visit back to Rochester, my thoughts began to conflict. Frankly, I hadn't expected Dr. M. to live as long as he had. It was all the excellent care he was receiving. I wish that was all there was to it, but God allowed him to survive—in part, to restore my heart and soul. I was such a sad girl when I met him, newly separated after twentyfive years of marriage, and now living a life full of total overwhelming responsibilities and cares. My children weighed heavily on my heart and mind. My daughter had cried so uncontrollably—shoulders going up and down kind of crying—when I left for the airport to return to England. I couldn't get that thought out of my head.

One week later, Dr. M. asked me what was wrong. He could sense something was amiss. So I shared my thoughts. He was quiet for what seemed like forever, thinking, I assume, for the correct response. Then, without showing emotion, he said, "You must go back to Rochester. I have a fine staff now, and I can do very well with Ufuk overseeing me along with Rose and the others. Make your plans."

Then he asked me, "Where are you going to live when you get back?" "Oh, I hadn't thought that far ahead yet," I said.

He then said, "Well, you can stay in my old house. It hasn't been sold, and you can pay me the rent."

I looked at him and initially rejected his offer out of pride or stupidity, but he wore me down and said, "Six hundred dollars per month." He made me sign an agreement, which impressed me—that he was still true to form with his thinking. I went ahead and organized my things to be sent back home. I didn't have much to pack because all my *monies went* toward flights. Well, I *did* learn to *travel on the cheap.* I've carried this skill with me to this day. You don't have to stay at the Ritz to see the sights and meet fabulous people along the way. Invaluable lessons. I always stay away from the main centers, which gives me a chance to walk and really take in the place. Now, if *I am* traveling with *another person,* I have to be more flexible, but it compensates because you can split the room rates. I have been so blessed in this season of my life with Dr. M.

As you know, I hate long goodbyes, and it couldn't have been truer than when I had to say goodbye to Dr. M.—my friend, my substitute father, my mentor. After I informed him that I was packed and ready to go in a week, he stunned me by asking, "Would you take me back to Rochester with you?" I gulped back the tears, but he knew this wasn't possible. His family had disappointed him, and vice versa. Too sad to be sure. I said goodbye to all my friends and assured them I would be back for visits. I instinctively knew I would never see Dr. M. alive again.

Homeward bound. It was a good flight, and I chatted with a woman next to me who was flying to NYC for the first time. She was from Romania and had opened a shoe shop for large-sized women's feet and wanted to check out the various shoes in the city. We will keep in touch. She has since become the headmaster of a Christian orphanage back home, and I still get Christmas cards from her and occasionally help her a little financially.

Now back home. The first thing I did was get a phone connected, as I had no cellphone. Remember those days? The second I stepped into the house, I dissolved into tears.

Dr. M. was not there, and yet he was. I called my son and then my daughter. "Hi, Mom, glad you're back," but it didn't sound convincing. I guess it would take some time for us all to adjust. My mother and dad were in Florida for the winter. I felt very alone.

I discovered mice in the basement—lots of them. I got busy straight away, ridding the house of them. The basement was waterproofed and painted. I didn't get my things out of storage because the house was a mess. Dr. M. said, "Go ahead and make any improvements you need to, but at your own expense." I had no job and no funds.

Dr. M. called one of his neurology friends, and they called and offered me a job at Strong Memorial Hospital in the Research Department. I could start tomorrow, which I did. After two weeks of onth0e- job training, I was asked to work the 3:00–11:30 p.m. shift. One RN and I covered a unit of nine beds. Because it was research, everything had to be weighed and measured—food and all other drinks in, and everything that came out as well. The research focused on patients with MS, MD, ALS, and diabetes, mostly. Dan was at his father's, in yet another new school system, and liked it, so working the evening shift worked well.

One evening, I arrived at work and was told the program was going to be put on hold. It seemed a med student had volunteered for a study that involved having a scope down her throat. She was given an anesthetic but had a very serious reaction. Protocols had to be reviewed and rewritten, which took time. In the meantime, we became an overflow unit. We started getting patients from the ED, postsurgical, OB/GYN—let's just say we had our noses stuck in the medical books before we'd agree we were prepared to accept any new patient. It worked for a time until it didn't.

After two days, I walked into Monroe Community Hospital, told them about my experience, and they hired me on the spot. I was assigned to the pediatric wing, where they had two children on ventilators. One charming seven-year-old had been hit by a car and was now unable to breathe on his own due to trauma. He was paralyzed from the neck down. I could take care of the elderly all day long—whatever they were dealing with, they had at least lived a life. Not so with children. I also cared for an infant, less than a year old, who was 100 percent brain-dead from shaken baby syndrome. The mother said the father did it, and the father said the mother did it. Not only had someone done this horrendous act to this beautiful, innocent child, but now the baby was also made to suffer, living in this state. No one could convince me that he didn't feel pain because when I had to turn him on his side, tears would slide down his cheek. Every night, I went home crying. I was, however, very grateful to be working and earning a paycheck.

I had enough money to purchase paint, and I painted the entire interior of the house by myself—off-white. I slept on an old twin mattress on the floor that I dragged down from upstairs and placed where Dr. M.'s bed used to be. It was cold and hollow-sounding in the house, but I was happy to be home.

Christmas came and went. I was now doing double shifts five days a week. I received a beautiful letter from Dr. M. at Christmas time, although it was generic and meant to go to many people throughout the world. Of course, Rose wrote it, but he dictated and somehow signed it. I sensed something was off in it. I called Mary, but she had gone to Ireland for the Christmas holiday. Dr. M. was not doing well, according to Ufuk. He had lost his appetite and was not eating. "Is he drinking his fluids?" I asked.

"No, not much."

I asked if I could speak to him, but I was told he was sleeping. He went downhill from there. I never got the full story. His doctor brother would not start an IV to give him fluids. When Rose came back from Ireland, she was upset to find him in this declined state. I called to speak to him, but she told me he could no longer speak. I asked her to put the phone up to his ear so I could speak to him. This was the first time I called him David. I was crying, trying to get a grip. I told him I loved him, was sorry I had left him, and asked him to forgive me. He tried to speak but could not. He died the following week.

What I thought and felt was that I had failed him. I have no other regrets in life but this one. I should have stayed. Why couldn't I have stayed until the end? I booked a flight to Heathrow and stepped into the church just in time for the funeral Mass to begin. The priest waited for me, bless him and those who knew I was on my way! Immediately following the service, we drove to his boyhood home, Lulworth Cove, for the burial. He was in a simple cardboard box, with no other containment, in an open dirt grave. Ashes to ashes, dust to dust. He was where he wanted to be. I had never met a man so humble with all that he had monetarily and the genuine friends who all but one came to visit him in the UK. Although he was raised Protestant, his father being a pastor, it was his friend, the priest at the hospital in Rochester, who gently drew him to become a Catholic. We had many discussions on this faith matter, as I was raised Catholic and became a born-again Christian believer.

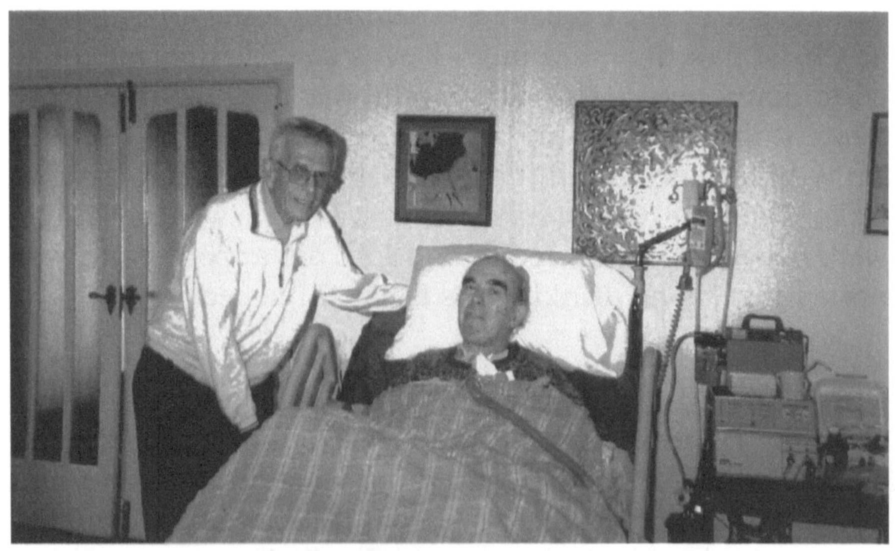

Father, priest friend of Dr. M.

Three months passed, and the phone rang. It was Dr. M.'s lawyer in the USA. He said, "Mary Susan?"

I said, "Yes, that's me."

He said, "I just want you to know that Dr. M. has willed you the house, free and clear. I'll send you the paperwork and the deed. Congratulations, well done."

Rest in peace, my dear Dr. David Marsh. I am truly blessed.

Sue and Dr. Marsh

About the Author

Mary Susan Cuminale has resided most of her life in Rochester, New York. She lived through the 1960s during the tragic assassinations of JFK, Robert Kennedy, and Martin Luther King Jr., as well as the Vietnam War. She married in 1969 and had two beautiful children and devoted herself to them. After twenty-five years, she was divorced. It was then she learned, over time, to become the self-sufficient woman she is today with God's help through the storms. Her journey continues.